Text copyright © Roy Apps 1997
Illustrations copyright © Nick Mountain 1997

First published in Great Britain in 1997
by Macdonald Young Books
an imprint of Wayland Publishers Ltd
61 Western Road
Hove
East Sussex
BN3 1JD

Find Macdonald Young Books on the internet at http://www.wayland.co.uk

Designed by Triggerfish, 11 Jew Street, Brighton, BN1 1UT
Printed and bound in Belgium by Proost International Book Production

British Library Cataloguing in Publication Data available

ISBN 0 7500 2371 6

SUPER SCIENTISTS

THE EXPLOSIVE DISCOVERY

ROY APPS

Illustrated by Nick Mountain

MACDONALD YOUNG BOOKS

Chapter 1

"You couldn't catch a flea and you can't catch me!"

I ran along the beach, my younger brothers and sisters racing after me. I darted behind my father's fishing boat.

"Maria!" Mama was in the boat, repairing nets.

"Come and sit down," she said. "I need to talk to you."

It sounded important.

I climbed into the boat and crouched down beside her.

Every winter, my mother would work as a maid for one of the rich villa owners who

came to our sunny seaside village of San
Remo for the winter months. Apart from the
little money my father earned fishing, that
was the only money we ever had.

"The winter visitors will soon be here,"
said my mother. "It will be time for *all* of us
womenfolk to find work."

"*All* of us womenfolk?"

I knew now what the important thing was that my mother wanted to tell me.

"Yes, Maria. You're thirteen. Old enough to start work."

And so it was that, a few weeks later, I found myself working as a maid in the house of a Swedish gentleman by the name of Señor Alfred Nobel.

Chapter 2

Señor Nobel
was not what
you would call a
cheerful man, but he
always seemed busy.
He spent most of the
time in his laboratory at the
end of the garden, surrounded
by bottles and flasks.

It was a mystery to me what exactly he got up to, but my little brother Emilio's friends said he was a wicked wizard.

The gossip among the grown ups was that he was one of the richest men in the world.

I was happy, though. I thought I had the best maid's job in San Remo.

Until one dreadful day.

"You are full of smiles this morning, Maria," Señor Nobel said.

"We all had a treat yesterday," I replied.

"We went up into the hills for a picnic.
It was my little brother Emilio's birthday.
He's my favourite brother, little Emilio.
Have you any brothers or sisters, Señor?"

I trailed off, as I saw Señor Nobel's face
suddenly turn red with anger.

"Stop it! Stop it! Do you dare mock me
in my own house?" he screamed.

He flung open the door. "Out!" he yelled.
"And don't ever come back!"

I needed no second bidding. I was out of the front gates and off down the road like a shot.

When I told my mother what had happened I didn't get any sympathy. "Your mouth is too big for your brain, you foolish child!" she scolded.

My father was furious, too. Particularly when he found out I'd run off from Señor Nobel's without collecting my wages.

"You go straight to the house tomorrow and ask him for the money, do you understand?"

"Yes, Papa."

I couldn't sleep. I was worried sick about going back to Señor Nobel's.

I still didn't know what I'd said or done to get myself dismissed like that.

What I did know was this: Señor Nobel was a troubled man.

Chapter 3

I woke to the sound of thunder.
The house seemed to be
shaking. Was it a thunderstorm
– or an earthquake?

I ran to the window.
The dawn sky was bright.
There was no storm; no
earthquake.

But there was a thin
pillar of smoke rising
from a large villa
overlooking
the sea.

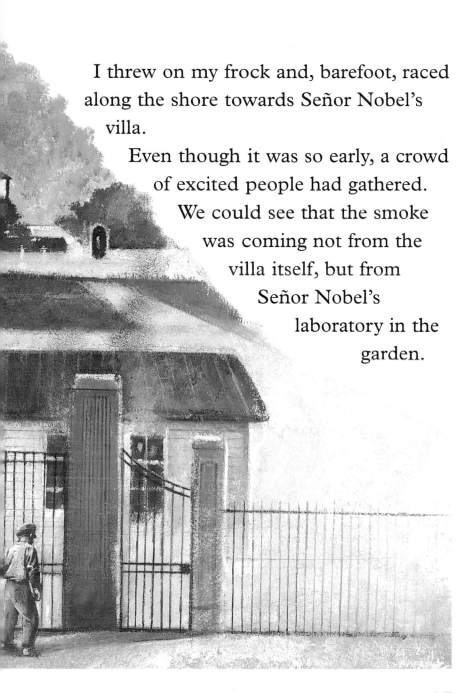

I threw on my frock and, barefoot, raced along the shore towards Señor Nobel's villa.

Even though it was so early, a crowd of excited people had gathered. We could see that the smoke was coming not from the villa itself, but from Señor Nobel's laboratory in the garden.

Señor Nobel's housekeeper ran out of the front door. She was carrying her bags.

"He's mad," she shrieked, pointing a stubby finger at her forehead. "A mad foreigner! He would have us all blown up! I'm not going to work in this place a minute longer!"

Some of the men helped her away with her bags.

The rest of the crowd began to edge away, talking excitedly to each other.

"He's not right in the head," they said.

"He should be locked up."

I saw Señor Nobel's worried face dart behind a curtain.

When I got back home, my mother's voice was firm. "You are never, *never* to go to that man's house again, do you hear me? Not even for the wages he owes you!"

I sat at the water's edge, drawing in the sand with a stick, while my little brother Emilio played with a bit of wood in the water, trying to get it to float.

"Maria?" A familiar, foreign voice called from behind me.

I spun round.

"Señor Nobel!"

"Your wages." He held out an envelope.

I took it and mumbled my thanks. It was strange, but he didn't seem in the least bit frightening now. In fact, he looked rather sad.

Did the accident in your workshop do much damage?" I asked.

It was a moment before he heard me. He was watching Emilio.

"Eh…? Oh no, no. Just one of those things…" He paused. "Maria. Would you come back and work for me?"

That's what he asked me! No mention of his outburst the day before.

"My parents wouldn't let me," I said.

"Not even if I offered to double your wages?"

I gulped.

"Papa says you're a wicked madman!" shrieked a small voice at my side. "He says you should be locked up!"

I'd been so busy talking to Señor Nobel that I hadn't seen Emilio come across to us.

"Emilio!" I reached out to box his ears. He ducked, but I managed to grab his shirt and struggled up in order to drag him off home.

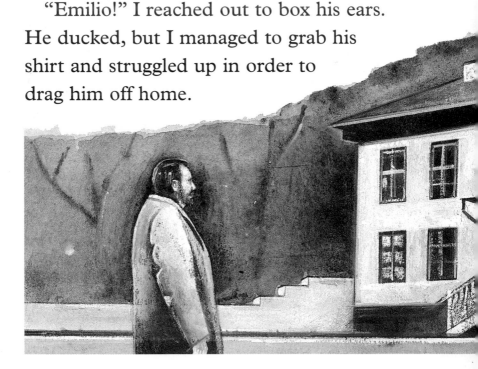

"So this is Emilio?" asked Señor Nobel.

I nodded, remembering that it had been my mention of Emilio that had sparked Señor Nobel's anger the day before.

He sighed. "Take care of him," he called after us.

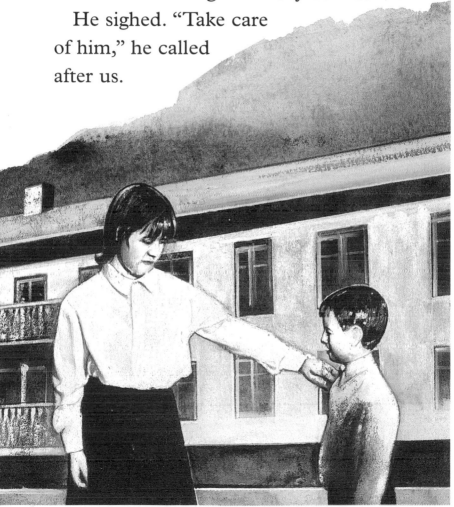

Chapter 4

"*Double* your wages?" My father's face was red with anger. "I wouldn't let you go back there, even if he offered you all the gold in the world. Even his housekeeper has left."

My mother looked him fully in the eye. "Of course she must go back! We can't turn that sort of money down."

"You'd send our daughter to work for that crazy foreigner?"

I looked from one to the other. They were talking about me as if I wasn't there!

"Have you got any other suggestions as to how we get enough money to live on?"

My father stormed out.

Only then did my mother turn to me.

"Nobody who offers double wages can be *that* bad," she said, with a twinkle in her eye.

"You know what he does in his laboratory? He's experimenting with things that blow up!" I said.

"Then don't go into his workshop, Maria," replied my mother, matter-of-factly.

I set off for Señor Nobel's the next day, my heart beating as fast as a bird's. It wasn't Señor Nobel's explosions I was afraid of, so much as his temper.

I was excited too, because it seemed to me that there was something very dark and mysterious about Señor Nobel.

I wanted to know what it was.

Chapter 5

That first day back I spent in a frenzy of cleaning, polishing, dusting, sweeping; all the time making sure I kept out of the "mad scientist's" way.

And so the days, the weeks went by. It was lonely work. Señor Nobel lived alone. There were no other servants in the villa; there were never any guests or visitors.

Each morning I would take a pot of coffee down the garden to his laboratory.

I would peer in and see all the rows of flasks and bottles, but I never went in. Whatever Señor Nobel's mystery was, I was sure the answer wasn't to be found in his laboratory.

Señor Nobel never lost
his temper again, though he
often asked about Emilio. Often
enough, in fact, for me to become convinced
that somehow my little brother was the key
to the mystery.

In the village, I became a bit of a heroine:
"There goes Maria," people would whisper.
"She's the girl who works for the madman
Nobel!"

One day, while I was dusting in Señor Nobel's office, I noticed that the top drawer of his desk was open.

In the drawer lay a very old photograph of two people standing by a large white house.

There was a young man in a suit – Señor Nobel, I could see that. The other figure was a boy of about my own age. He was dark, smiling and so handsome.

I picked up the photograph to have a closer look.

Suddenly, I heard the back door bang. Quickly, I tried to put the photograph back in the drawer, but I was flustered and to my horror, the photograph slipped through my fingers and fluttered to the floor.

Even as I hurriedly stooped down to pick it up, I felt a large shadow loom over me. I looked up. "I'm sorry, Señor Nobel," I mumbled.

"The drawer was open..."

He took the photograph from me without speaking. I waited for him to shout at me – to tell me to get out.

But he didn't.

He just stared long and hard at it and I knew that any anger he might have felt had melted away.

Instead, he looked up at me with sad, far-away eyes. "Let me tell you a story, Maria," he said.

Chapter 6

"You know by now the nature of my experiments," Señor Nobel said.

I nodded.

"Explosives was my father's business, also. With him and my younger brother, I set up a small factory near Stockholm, in my country, Sweden."

I nodded again.

"For a year all went well, and we sold nitroglycerine…"

I must have frowned.

"… an oily substance; highly explosive. We sold it for quarrying and mining. Then one September day, something went terribly wrong. There was a huge, violent explosion…"

"Like the one in your laboratory the other week?" I suggested.

Señor Nobel shook his head. "This explosion rocked the whole factory and shook houses nearby."

I shuddered.

"Five people were killed. Four of them factory workers..."

Señor Nobel paused.

"And the fifth?" I asked.

"My younger brother, Emil."

I didn't need to say anything else. I knew that the young boy in the photograph was Señor Nobel's brother, Emil.

I knew too, why he had been so upset when I had asked him if he had any brothers and sisters. And why he was so interested in my own little brother, Emilio.

I knew now the mystery of Señor Nobel.

"Emil was my favourite brother," Señor Nobel went on, quietly. He was still looking at the photograph.

"I'm so sorry," I said.

Señor Nobel laid the photograph on the table.

"There was uproar in the town. Every time I ventured on to the street I was jostled, spat at even. 'Murderer!' they screamed at me.

"They paraded outside the factory, demanding that the town council close it down. And so they did. We had nowhere to go. In the end we had to open our new factory on an old barge on Lake Malar.

"Since that day I have worked solidly. It is easier to forget when you are working."

"Carrying on making explosives?"
Señor Nobel nodded. "But safer
explosives. I discovered that by mixing
nitroglycerine with a very porous form of
clay, called Kieselguhr, it is a lot safer to
handle. If only I'd made my discovery
a few years earlier, my little brother
would still be alive…"

Señor Nobel trailed off. Then he shrugged and strode back towards the door.

"I don't know why I'm troubling you with all this…the sad thoughts of an old man," he said.

I smiled gently, but said nothing.

I knew the answer to his question though: he had no one else to tell.

Chapter 7

After that, Señor Nobel and I often used to talk. I'd tell him all the local gossip. One day I even told him about Enzo, the boy who had started coming to the villa to walk me home from work.

Señor Nobel would tell me about the oil shipping business he'd run with his older brothers. Fifty three oil tankers he'd owned at one time, some of them weighing five thousand tonnes! Even Papa was impressed when I told him that.

There was one thing though that Señor
Nobel kept coming back to: dynamite.

One day, he said, "sometimes I wish I'd
never invented such a terrible thing."

"But dynamite is very useful, Señor! Look
how engineers have been able to blast
through the Alps to build a railway! They
couldn't have done that without dynamite."

Señor Nobel shook his head slowly.

"Maybe. But it is also a terrible weapon of war."

"Well, you can't *un-invent* it, Señor," I shrugged.

"When I am gone, I shall be remembered as the man who made bombs. That's what they call me now."

"They also call you one of the richest men in the world," I replied. For a moment, I thought he was going to tell me off for my cheekiness.

But he just nodded, slowly.

"What I mean is," I went on, "you could leave something else for the future..."

Without another word, Señor Nobel left the room and went to his study.

And I went about my work.

Señor Nobel never talked to me about dynamite again.

Chapter 8

I worked for Señor Nobel for two more
winters, until I married Enzo and we moved
away from San Remo to another village
further down the coast.

A few years later I saw the newspaper headline: "Death in San Remo of Señor Alfred Nobel". I remember the day well, it was the day my second son was born.

Later, when I heard about Nobel Prizes for science and medicine, literature and peace, I recalled my words to Señor Nobel – "you could leave something else for the future".

I watched my two children running along the water's edge.

I was glad that we had christened the elder one Emilio, but I was even gladder that we had christened the younger one Alfredo.

Timeline

Alfred Nobel was born on 21 October 1833 in Stockholm, Sweden.

1842	The Nobel family moves to St Petersburg, Russia.
1850	Nobel leaves Russia, able to speak five languages fluently. He spends four years working in the United States.
1863	Nobel and his father open their first nitroglycerine factory.
1864	Alfred's brother, Emil, is killed in an explosion at the Nobel nitroglycerine factory. Alfred experiments with ways to make nitroglycerine safe to handle.
1867	Nobel is granted a patent for dynamite in Britain. This means that no one can steal his idea.

1876	Nobel patents a stronger type of dynamite – blasting gelatin.
1891	Nobel leaves France to live in Italy. He stays in San Remo for some time.
1901	The first Nobel Prizes, for Physics, Chemistry, Physiology or Medicine, Literature and Peace, are awarded, five years after Nobel's death.

Alfred Nobel died on 10 December 1896 in San Remo, Italy. He was 63 years old.

Glossary

detonator	a piece of equipment used to set off an explosion
dynamite	a type of explosive
explosives	mixtures of chemicals which can blow up, or explode. They can be used to cause damage, injure people, blow away rock or stone and demolish buildings.
minerals	coal, iron ore and tin are minerals found beneath the earth's surface
mining	digging deep below the ground to find minerals or precious metals
nitroglycerine	a type of explosive
porous	a substance full of tiny holes, which liquids can pass through easily
quarrying	when minerals are dug from the earth's surface. Explosives can be used to blow away the top layer of earth to reveal the minerals beneath.

If you have enjoyed this Storybook, why not try these other titles in the Super Scientists series:

The Mysterious Element by Pam Robson

Marie Curie was a very unusual scientist – a woman! Determined to prove that she is as good as a man, she earns two university degrees, before embarking on her most exciting adventure – the search for radium.

Heavens Above by Kenneth Ireland

Galileo Galilei has had a brilliant idea for a telescope – the only problem is, someone else thought of it first! And as for his ideas about the Earth travelling around the Sun... The Pope is not amused.

The Bright Idea by Ann Moore

Thomas Edison is *always* busy in his laboratory. His daughter Marion decides to find out exactly what he's doing in there and witnesses one of Edison's greatest achievements – the light bulb!

The Cosmic Professor by Andrew Donkin

Eddie can't believe that he's met *Albert Einstein*, the most famous professor in the world. And he's amazed when Einstein offers to explain the secrets of the universe. Is Outer Space all it seems?

The Colour of Light by Meredith Hooper

What is light and what colour is it? *Isaac Newton* isn't sure, but he wants to find out. So he buys a prism, holds it up to a beam of light and a wonderful rainbow shimmers before his eyes... What *can* this mean?

Storybooks are available from your local bookshop or can be ordered direct from the publishers. For more information about storybooks, write to: *The Sales Department, Macdonald Young Books, 61 Western Road, Hove, East Sussex, BN3 1JD.*